The River

AN EROTIC STORY

WRITTEN BY SUNDARI GRACE
ILLUSTRATIONS BY PEARLY L

© Sundari Grace 2019
First published in Australia in 2020 as this edition.

ISBN: 978-0-6485533-8-0 (Paperback)
ISBN: 978-0-6485533-9-7 (Hardcover)

All rights reserved. Apart from any fair dealing for the purposes of private study, research, criticism or review, as permitted under copyright law, no part of this book may be reproduced by any process without written permission. Inquiries should be addressed to info@sundarigrace.com.

Cover artwork and illustrations by Pearly L.

www.sundarigrace.com

For all the Feminines and Masculines
who are learning love that liberates.

HER

As I neared the river, I saw him throwing a blanket out wide over the soft grass, like it would spread far enough to cover the world. Half-naked, no shoes, skin shining in response to the blazing sun, he carefully laid out items like plans and I arrived at a completed scene, already opening.

He smiled at me and took me in his arms and hovered his lips close to mine, barely touching as his whispered 'Hello my beautiful one' flowed through me like a rolling wind and I lost the lines of my body and felt myself grass and oxygen and the warmth of a near sky.

HIM

My heart left my body and entered hers as she relaxed into those first, gentle waves of orgasm that always served to initiate my undoing. I marvelled again how easily, given the right love, she would come. I drew my attention to focus, poured presence into my muscles like strength to hold her firm so she was free not to.

She smiled at me, brought her lips over mine and kissed me and I invited her to climb inside my chest, pulling her heart to me like it could replace my own. Using the flow of presence through my body, I lifted her feet off the ground and carried her towards the river.

HER

My feet landed on the rock more softly than seemed possible, the carefulness in his arms denying gravity, his forethought providing the folded blanket that cushioned the hardness of stone. We were in the river but the rock held us above the water, our skin teased by the river's giant auric flow that felt like ethereal silk.

He removed our clothing, piece by piece, peeling away the layers of civilisation that, here, felt like the toxic residue of things gone wrong and our bodies breathed in the rich, fresh air through every skin cell.

HIM

I threw the bundle of clothes aside with a movement that threw my hand too quickly into her energy field and her body jerked away from me with sudden, heart-breaking tension. I schooled my body to steadiness and presence and gently drew her to me.

Tension drained from her with a delight that sounded like the trickling of the river over the rocks and her body became fluid also and moved to my direction as I sat us both down on the cushioned rock and I turned her to face the oncoming river.

HER

The river's energy came at me and pressed me back into his chest and down into his lap and I was moulded to him and caught in the beautiful hold of river and lover and their sweet, conscious collusion. I became at once one with the water, the rush of energy and air and the beautiful man behind me.

I could feel him preparing, readying for something that was yet unmade and waiting until I was ready also. My torso broadened with gratitude for the trustworthiness he held out to me on an open heart, that shaped my anticipation as arousal instead of fear, and I giggled as electricity tickled from perineum to crown. His bared hands filled with my thighs and in one swift but steady motion, he lifted me and parted my legs to the river.

HIM

Her whole body rolled like a wave over and over again, moved by the rolling river's energy flowing into her, through her and out through her Queen crown. I held her safe but free, draped over me but lifting to the sky till I felt her float above the earth, drawing me with her past the canopy of trees and out into infinite space.

My heart, inside her, felt worlds-wide and growing, overtaking identity and fear and exploding both into the stars that surround us on all sides now. Perhaps we journeyed for hours - who, re-becoming the Universe, can tell?

More by Sundari Grace

Trust, Sex, Heights & Enlightenment
Magic Blood: A loving reminder

About the Author

Originally from Melbourne, Australia, Sundari Grace has lived in Australia, the USA and Chile and now resides in sunny south-east Queensland. She started writing poetry and short stories in her early teens and has been on a lifelong journey of discovery ever since.

Sundari's writing reflects her deep and abiding interest in spirituality, sex and relationships as extreme sports that challenge and empower us to grow.

She explores the light and shadow self, and the adventure of showing up in both – in solitude and interaction – to create opportunities to self-actualise and support each other to do so. Key themes in her writing include explorations of yearning, spiritual concepts of feminine/masculine, nature, beauty, energy, power and choice.

She draws on exploration and study in the fields of spirituality and literature, and is inspired by any experience that feels like jumping out of a plane.

www.ingramcontent.com/pod-product-compliance
Lightning Source LLC
Chambersburg PA
CBHW041431010526
44107CB00046B/1571